June

Gavin,

Hopefully you will record a little 'bit' about your trips — and enjoy the memories for a long long time!

Love,

Mom

P.S. We are on route to San Jose where Gavin will fly to visit Vanessa in Seattle & Gran + Pops' in Vancouver!

Travel

NOTES

9 8
Digit on the right indicates the number of this printing.

ISBN 1–56138–582–4

Cover design by Toby Schmidt
Cover and interior illustrations by Valerie Coursen
Interior design by Frances J. Soo Ping Chow
Edited by William King
Typography by Justin T. Scott
Printed in the United States

This book may be ordered by mail from the publisher.
Please add $1.00 for postage and handling.
But try your bookstore first!

Running Press Book Publishers
125 South Twenty-second Street
Philadelphia, Pennsylvania 19103–4399

Travel

NOTES

RUNNING PRESS
PHILADELPHIA · LONDON

*J*ourneys. Even the word sounds as if it has been drawn from some magic elixir and distilled through the gossamer screen of the imagination.

PHYLLIS TAYLOR PIANKA
20TH-CENTURY AMERICAN WRITER

6/16

Today I'm going
home from Vancouver,
on the Bus (greyhound).
I left this morning
at 9:30, got on the sea
Bus, then the sky train
to the greyhound station.
I gave gram a kiss
and a hugg and left.
It

The simple fact seems to have been that once I saw that mysterious road outside my house, the eastern part leading to a dead end, the western to worlds unknown, I was determined to explore the latter.

James A. Michener (1907–1997)
American writer

Writing gives me an excuse to travel,

and travel gives me something to write about.

Athena V. Lord (b. 1932)
American writer

Not traveling is like living in the Library of Congress
but never taking out more than one or two books.

For my part, I travel not to go anywhere, but to go.
I travel for travel's sake. The great affair is to move.

Robert Louis Stevenson (1850–1894)
Scottish writer

Traveling tends to magnify all human emotions.

Whenever we left . . . the latent feelings of love, friendship,

and animosity would all explode.

Peter Hoeg (b. 1957)
Dutch writer

An agreeable companion on a journey

is as good as a carriage.

PUBLILIUS SYRUS
1ST CENTURY B.C.
ROMAN WRITER

*N*ever go on trips with anyone you do not love.

Ernest Hemingway (1899–1961)
American writer

Why do people so love to wander? I think the civilized parts of the World will suffice for me in the future.

Mary Cassatt (1844–1926)
American painter

Each journey is an experience of the past. . . .

Robert Vetter
20th-century American anthropologist

. . . to go from here to there, to travel in the most remote regions

is like winding up a time machine or turning on the tape recorder

that all of us carry around in our heads.

Luisa Valenzuela (b. 1938)
Argentinean writer

*T*o travel is to take a journey into yourself.

Dena Kaye
20th-century American writer

You lose sight of things . . . and when you travel,
everything balances out.

DARANNA GIDEL (B. 1948)
AMERICAN WRITER

When I travel, my eyes are arrested by detail. I do not give up my mind to the whole. I listen to the impressions which burst from my personal reaction.

Anaïs Nin (1903–1977)
French-born American writer

As we travel around today we see that our Mother Earth is still doing

her duty, and for that we are very grateful.

Irving Powless, Sr.,
20th-century
Native American (Onondaga) Chief

*O*ur happiest moments as tourists always seem to come when we stumble upon one thing while in pursuit of something else.

Lawrence Block (b. 1938)
American novelist

Yet the good traveller, even now, need not find himself alienated.
Everywhere he can discover . . . oases and enclaves
of his own culture. . . .

JAN MORRIS (B. 1926)
ENGLISH WRITER

Traveling is seeing; *it is the implicit that we travel by.*

Cynthia Ozick (b. 1931)
American writer

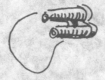

Value the intangibles of travel—they are treasures
that are more beautiful than gold or diamonds.

ALEXANDRA STODDARD
20TH-CENTURY AMERICAN WRITER

. . . traveling . . . is either an escape or a discovery.

Rosie Thomas (b. 1947)
English writer

Rather than view travel as
an escape from everyday reality,
we might try viewing it as an escape
back into a time-honored — and
perhaps more realistic — human
rhythm. . . .

Doug Chadwick
20th-century American writer

Why, it would really be being unselfish to go away and be happy for a little, because we would come back so much nicer. You see, after a bit everybody needs a holiday.

MARY A. ARNIM (1866–1941)
ENGLISH WRITER

*T*ravel in the younger sort is
a part of education, in the elder
a part of experience.

Francis Bacon (1561–1626)
English philosopher

All travel has its advantages. If the passenger visits better countries,
he may learn to improve his own, and if fortune carries him to
worse, he may learn to enjoy it.

Samuel Johnson (1709–1784)
English writer

. . . the seasoned traveler accepts the surprises and inconveniences
which are an inevitable part of any trip.

Jane Stanton Hitchcock
20th-century American writer and dramatist

Travel teaches toleration.

Benjamin Disraeli (1804–1881)
English statesman and writer

. . . it is every traveler's conceit that no
one will see what he has seen: his trip
displaces the landscape and his version
of events is all that matters.

PAUL THEROUX (B. 1941)
AMERICAN WRITER

*A*mericans have always been eager for travel, that being how they got to the New World in the first place.

Otto Friedrich (b. 1929)
American journalist

For every traveller who has any taste of his own,
the only useful guide-book will be the one
which he himself has written.

ALDOUS HUXLEY (1894–1963)
ENGLISH WRITER

When lost, I look for gas stations for counsel.

Laurel Lee (b. 1945)
American writer

I always rely on scenery to deaden the inconvenience of travel. . . .

Richard Powers (b. 1957)
American writer

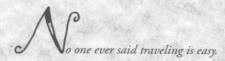

No one ever said traveling is easy.

Lilian Jackson Braun (b. 1916)
American writer

In the space age, man will be
able to go around the world in two
hours — one for flying and the
other to get to the airport.

Neil H. McElroy (1904–1972)
U.S. Secretary of Defense

Why endeavor to straighten the road of life?

The faster we travel, the less there is to see.

Helen Hayes (1900–1993)
American actress

After a journey, first impressions of familiar places are as strange as what one left home to experience.

EVELYN AMES
20TH-CENTURY AMERICAN WRITER

My own journey started long before I left, and was over
before I returned.

John Steinbeck (1902–1968)
American writer

For myself, indeed, I know now that I have traveled so much
because travel has enabled me to arrive at new, unknown places
within my own clouded self.

LAUREN VAN DER POST (B. 1906)
SOUTH AFRICAN WRITER

But do not hurry the journey at all.

Better that it should last many years;

Be quite old when you anchor at the island,

Rich with all you have gained on the way,

Not expecting Ithaka to give you riches.

Constantine Carafy (1863–1933)
Greek poet

There is one voyage, the first, the last, the only one.

Thomas Wolfe (1900–1938)
American writer